GARDEN POOL DESIGN

by Helmut Jantra

Originally published in German under the title *Gartenteiche gestalten.* © 1993 by Franckh-Kosmos Verlags-GmbH & Co., Stuttgart.

Copyright © 1994 by T.F.H. Publications, Inc. for the English-language edition. A considerable amount of new material, including but not limited to additional photographs, has been added to the literal German/English translation; copyright is also claimed for this new material.

1995 Edition

Distributed in the UNITED STATES to the Pet Trade by T.F.H. Publications, Inc., One T.F.H. Plaza, Neptune City, NJ 07753; distributed in the UNITED STATES to the Bookstore and Library Trade by National Book Network, Inc. 4720 Boston Way, Lanham MD 20706; in CANADA to the Pet Trade by H & L Pet Supplies Inc., 27 Kingston Crescent, Kitchener, Ontario N2B 2T6; Rolf C. Hagen Ltd., 3225 Sartelon Street, Montreal 382 Quebec; in CANADA to the Book Trade by Vanwell Publishing Ltd., 1 Northrup Crescent, St. Catharines, Ontario L2M 6P5 ; in ENGLAND by T.F.H. Publications, PO Box 15, Waterlooville PO7 6BQ; in AUSTRALIA AND THE SOUTH PACIFIC by T.F.H. (Australia), Pty. Ltd., Box 149, Brookvale 2100 N.S.W., Australia; in NEW ZEALAND by Brooklands Aquarium Ltd. 5 McGiven Drive, New Plymouth, RD1 New Zealand; in Japan by T.F.H. Publications, Japan—Jiro Tsuda, 10-12-3 Ohjidai, Sakura, Chiba 285, Japan; in SOUTH AFRICA by Lopis (Pty) Ltd., P.O. Box 39127, Booysens, 2016, Johannesburg, South Africa. Published by T.F.H. Publications, Inc.
MANUFACTURED IN THE UNITED STATES OF AMERICA
BY T.F.H. PUBLICATIONS, INC.

BAMBOO POND WITH SPRING

This idyllic 40-square-meter pond is dominated by an over four-meter-high green wall of the bamboo species *Phyllostachys aurea*; it occupies the side of the pond opposite the bench. Because of the pond's naturally curved form and the dense border planting with ornamental shrubs, it looks almost enchanted. The right side is enclosed by a *Thuja* hedge. Neither the hedge nor the two Japanese maples in the vicinity of a barberry are obtrusive in any way. Two artificial elements, a Chinese stone lantern and a Balinese temple dancer in crouching posture, also fit harmoniously into the over-all picture.

The two Japanese maples *(Acer palmatum)* are in clear view on a small pile of large stones from which water raised by a submersible pump splashes down. This part of the pond as well as a large percentage of the

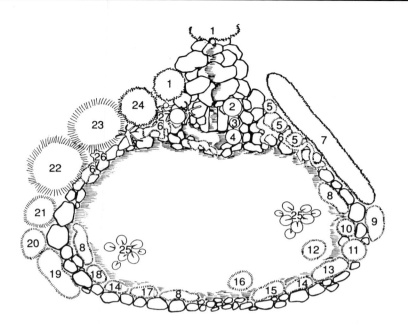

remaining area is deliberately kept free of floating plants so as not to detract from the reflection of the water. Water lilies and yellow pond lilies have been established near the water's edge on either side of the bench.

Also growing here in small containers are pickerel weed (Pontederia cordata), arrowhead (Sagittaria sagittifolia), pygmy cattail (Typha minima), and common mare's tail (Hippuris vulgaris), while frogbit (Hydrocharis morsus-ranae) and water soldier (Stratiotes aloides) are free floating. Hair grass (Eleocharis acicularis) and water violet (Hottonia palustris) were chosen as submerged plants.

The focal points of the border planting are located in the front at the water's edge with tulips and other flowering bulbs, which are subsequently relieved by annual summer blooms, and on either side of the waterfall on the spring mound. Alongside ferns in the shade of the maples and bamboo, it is mainly creeping Jenny (Lysimachia nummularia) that sends its strings of foliage over the large stones. Special features include a house fern, child's head (Soleirolia soleirolii), and a giant-leaved Colocasia gigantea from Java, which are not winter-hardy and spend the summer here in their pots.

POND WITH WATERFALL AND ISLAND

The approximately ten-meter-long pond edged with massive granite blocks can fill a large part of a garden. The slope from the raised house terrace was transformed here into a "rock face" for water trickling down from above.

During excavation a small area was retained as an island, on which there is room for a large, five-armed candelabra, a huge Chinese reed *(Miscanthus sinensis)*, and two bronze herons with an underplanting of ornamental grasses. Three pools are formed in the rocky wall, in which the water collects and is dispersed as it continues to flow down. These pools also serve as sites for bog plants in pots, which break up the monotony of the visually dominant rock formation.

Because the rear part of the pond is hidden from the observer by the island, the visible water surface should be kept as free of plant growth as possible. The planting is therefore limited to several water lilies in containers.

The pond's edge has individually laid natural flagstones, between which grow small pulvinate perennials, such as various *Sempervivum* hybrids (Houseroot). Houseroot, hens and chicks (*Sedum* species), breakstone *(Saxifraga),* and basket of gold *(Alyssum)* also

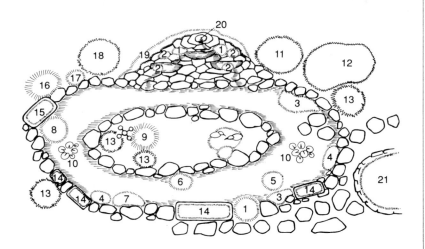

1. Fern; 2. bog plants; 3. cattail *(Typha)*; 4. common mare's tail *(Hippuris vulgaris)*; 5. *Colocasia*; 6. umbrella plant *(Cyperus)*; 7. pickerel weed *(Pontederia cordata)*; 8. New Zealand flax *(Phormium tenax)*; 9. giant Chinese reed *(Miscanthus sinensis)*; 10. water lily; 11. false cypress *(Thuja)*; 12. pine; 13. Japanese maple *(Acer palmatum)*; 14. planted trough; 15. table garden; 16. bamboo; 17. *Yucca*; 18. hemlock *(Tsuga)*; 19. willow grass *(Polygonum)*; 20. spring stone; 21. Stone wall with garden plants.

populate several stone troughs on the sides of the pond.

In order for a majority of the rocky wall to be covered with trickling water, it was necessary to install two submersible pumps serving two spray heads, which were also hidden behind large rocks. This pool, ás well as the previously described installation (***Bamboo Pond with Spring, page 2),*** was constructed with flexible liners, the seams of which were glued together by the dealer according to predetermined dimensions.

The water is trickling over the rocky wall. Two submersible pumps are required.

WATER GARDEN WITH SEVERAL POOLS

It does not necessarily require a large area to group an ensemble of three differently designed and shaped pools. A water garden of this kind could consist, for example, of a pre-shaped pool, a round pool with a flexible liner, and a plastic container about 60 centimeters in diameter sunk at ground level. With this water garden the backdrop is again defined by tall bamboo which can be substituted for just as well by less dominating ornamental shrubs. As a floor covering between the pools, small square flagstones were chosen, which fit in well in the very natural-appearing installation. A large plantain lily bordering the flagstones serves to break up the monotony and feels quite at home in the humidity of the neighboring water despite the predominantly sunny site.

The center of the round pool with the liner is adorned by a sandstone slab that rests on a foundation hidden underwater. The slab has a hole bored in the middle, through which trickles water conveyed by a submersible pump. The front part of the pool has a bed of gravel, which

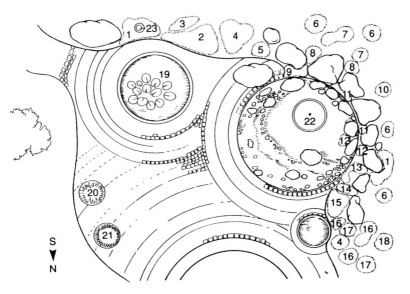

1. Daylily; 2. centaurea; 3. gayfeather; 4. spiderwort; 5. Japanese maple; 6. bamboo; 7. tickseed; 8. jasmine; 9. Japanese primrose; 10. sea kale; 11. sensitive fern; 12. sweet galingale; 13. Siberian iris; 14. drumstick primula; 15. plantain lily; 16. false dragonhead; 17. lamp cleaner grass; 18. dogwood; 19. water lily; 20. Indian arrowroot; 21. umbrella grass and milfoil; 22. spring stone; 23. lamp. Underplanting with *Viola sorroria* "Immaculata," *Brunnera macrophylla,* and *Duchesnea indica.*

merges into the large pebbles on the pool's edge.

Whereas the pre-shaped pool to the left has almost disappeared under a carpet of water lily leaves, in contrast, the surface of the round pool is kept entirely free of floating aquatic plants. The sunken container on the right is reserved for two red-eared turtles, which are transferred in winter to the deeper pre-shaped pool.

The entire installation is edged by a low mound of earth, which serves as a planting bed for numerous low to medium-high perennials, spring-blooming bulbs, and colorful summer flowers. The relatively dense growth serves to unify the three ponds and to make them appear as a visual whole.

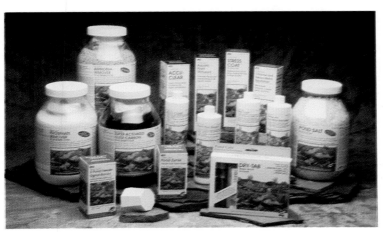

Many fine products are available for conditioning and treating the water in a pool—very important considerations in the health of the pool's inhabitants. Photo courtesy of Aquarium Pharmaceuticals.

WATER GARDEN WITH WOOD DECK

In the place of a covering of flagstones, wooden slats are used here. The corners project over the water, creating the illusion of being on a footbridge above the water's surface and experiencing an "island effect." If the deck extends only a short distance into the pond area, it can be supported on stone footings that can be anchored securely in the vegetation-covered soil at the water's edge. If the wooden deck is cantilevered far over the water, the supporting elements must rest directly on a footing set on the bottom of the pond.

Depending on the size of the pond, either several decks with different patterns of lathing or a single larger surface that can simultaneously serve as a place to sit over the water can be chosen. This design is suitable for a so-called cottage garden, and will not conflict with a more modern installation because of its geometric form.

Where so much wood dominates, special attention should be paid to both the planting and to breaking up the monotony of the view, which tends to be somewhat static and barren. One possibility is a large bog garden, in which taller-growing plants of shallow water, such as the flowering rush (*Butomus umbellatus*), purple loosestrife (*Lythrum salicaria*), bulrush (*Scirpus lacustris*), or yellow flag (*Iris pseudacorus*), have a place.

If there is enough room, potted plants in suitable terra-cotta containers can liven things up. Suitable candidates include umbrella grass (*Cyperus alternifolius*) or the huge, decorative New Zealand flax (*Phormium tenax*), of which there are several interesting varieties.

1. Bulrush (*Scirpus lacustris*); 2. golden club (*Orontium aquaticum*); 3. plantain lily (*Hosta*); 4. bog bean (*Menyanthes trifoliata*); 5. daylily (*Hemerocallis*); 6. marsh marigold (*Caltha palustris*); 7. Schaublatt (*Rodgersia*); 8. purple loosestrife (*Lythrum salicaria*); 9. yellow flag (*Iris pseudacorus*); 10. Joe-Pye weed (*Eupatorium*); 11. flowering rush (*Butomus umbellatus*); 12. inula (*Inula magnifica*); 13. ligularia (*Ligularia*); 14. water plantain (*Alisma plantago-aquatica*); 15. water lily; 16. lamp. The dotted line shows the outline of the liner under the wooden deck. In this way it is possible to see the water through the individual wooden slats.

1. Bench; 2. Joe-Pye weed (*Eupatorium*); 3. lady's mantle (*Alchemilla*); 4. spiderwort (*Tradescantia X Andersoniana* hybrids); 5. Siberian iris (*Iris sibirica*); 6. globe flower (*Trollius europaeus*); 7. purple loosestrife (*Lythrum salicaria*); 8. tickseed (*Coreopsis tripteris*); 9. monks hood (*Aconitum*); 10. meadow rue (*Thalictrum flavum*); 11. garden spirea (*Astilbe*); 12. snakeroot (*Cimicifuga*); 13. daylily (*Hemerocallis* in varieties); 14. plantain lily (*Hosta* in varieties); 15. geum (*Geum rivale*); 16. hazel;

WATER GARDEN WITH BRIDGE OR STEPPING STONES

Prefabricated bridges in a multitude of sizes and models are available from lumber yards, home centers, specialized mail-order houses, and sometimes large garden centers. However, there is always the danger of miscalculating the dimensions by buying something too big and being stuck with an object that is out of proportion to the garden pond and its surroundings. Particularly with a smaller body of water, it can be visually more pleasing to pick a simple, massive tree trunk secured over the water instead of a conspicuous bridge. In any case, it is important to provide a stable mooring on the two banks, such as on a concrete footing sunk into the ground.

For a shallow pond or a small stream, stepping stones make a nice substitute for a bridge. They not only look natural, but invite the visitor to linger and take a closer look at the life in the water. These stepping stones can also lead to an inviting seat on the other side of the pond. If they are only to be used for their visual effect, large natural stone blocks are well suited. They will become covered with moss in the course of time and take on an ancient appearance, as if

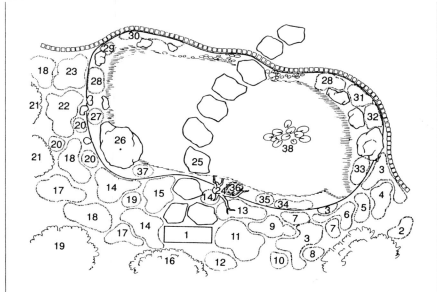

17. phlox; 18. Beinwell (*Symphytum grandiflorum*); 19. (*Prunus*); 20. sedge (*Carex pendula*); 21. bamboo (*Sinarundinaria*); 22. aster (*Aster divaricatus*); 23. alkanet (*Brunnera macrophylla*); 24. root; 25. stepping stone; 26. splash fountain, *Bog*; 27. bulrush (*Scirpus lacustris*); 28. marsh marigold (*Caltha palustris*); 29. hair grass (*Eleocharis acicularis*); 30. rose primula (*Primula rosea*); 31. Japanese primula (*Primula japonica*); 32. American yellow flag (*Iris versicolor*); 33. sweet galingale (*Cyperus longus*); 34. water plantain (*Alisma plantago-aquatica*); 35. yellow flag (*Iris pseudacorus*); 36. bog kidney fern (*Thelypteris palustris*); 37. flowering rush (*Butomus umbellatus*); 38. water lily.

they had always rested there.

If they are to be used to cross the water area, a slip-resistant and stable material, such as natural or artificial stone slabs, must be used. They should be attached to a stable footing with silicone cement. Too great a distance between the individual steps should be avoided since they might force you to cross too quickly!

Setting the stepping stones in a curve instead of a straight line can look more attractive and can make a larger portion of the pond's surface accessible. This is also an advantage for planting, care, and cleaning.

Instead of a bridge, a constricted section which allows you to step over the pond can be used.

Illustration on facing page: pond with summer flowers.

POND WITH SUMMER FLOWERS

This is one possible design for smaller pre-shaped pools or pools with liners where, perhaps because of a lack of space, an extensive planting of the margins is impossible **(see below for illustration).**

You may also want to use every bit of available space for colorful summer flowers, but want to have running water too. From a distance this area will look like a large flower bed, and only on closer approach will what is hidden behind it be discovered. Even a three- or four-meter-long pre-shaped pool is well suited for this purpose. It can be surrounded by tall and short student flowers *(Tagetes)*, multi-colored hardworking Elizabeth in colorful mixtures, snapdragons, zinnias, salvias, and Goldmohn, which are best planted in groupings of complementary colors. These temperamental shades are toned down a bit by silverleaf *(Senecio bicolor)* planted between them in clumps or on the margins. If the pool is surrounded by slightly overhanging, reddish yellow sandstone flagstones, nothing will look artificial.

The next step would be the addition of an adjoining bog garden with tall common mare's tail *(Hippuris vulgaris)* and pygmy cattail *(Typha minima)*, which can likewise be set off from the main pond with sandstone slabs or large gravel. Such a "blooming water island" also fits in well on the edge or in the middle of an ornamental lawn, where it draws attention to itself. According to taste, the water's surface can be further animated by a water lily or bubbler fountain, and there would be no objection to a few goldfish either. Such summer-flowering plants have the advantage that the composition can be varied from year to year.

Illustration on facing page: geometric pool.

THE GEOMETRIC POOL

Geometric pools are those with strict linearity, with a square or quadratic form. Angled models or T-shapes also involve this concept, as well as a round pool. *(For an illustration of a finished geometric pool, see below.)*

Water gardens of this kind are suitable for modern bungalows with areas of lawn laid out in geometric form or the courtyard of an atrium, when they, for example, are sunk at the level of a covering of flagstones. In this case a sparse planting with a few water lilies will be chosen, increased attention will be given to the immediate surroundings, and plants in suitable decorative pots and containers

will be selected; they accentuate the southern character of the installation, which lends a touch of Moorish horticulture or echoes of Tuscan gardens of the 16th Century.

If you would like to keep it simpler, sink a rectangular or angled pre-shaped pool in a suitable space slightly below ground level and use tiles or flagstones to cover the edges, following the strict linearity of the pool. The planting of the adjoining bed will be determined by the available space, the plants, and the style of the rest of the garden. It can look very elegant here when the planting is limited to a few decorative ornamental shrubs, such as mahonia, rhododendron, spirea, or red-twigged dogwood.

Of course, one does not have to adhere to strict symmetry in the making of the pond. If, for example, the margins are lined with the aforementioned natural flagstones and the rear part of the marginal area is built up into a flat mound or turned into a rock garden, a natural-appearing wet biotope can still be created. It will not appear any less attractive in comparison to a natural pond.

THE POND ON THE TERRACE SLOPE

This interesting solution is apparently rarely encountered because it is difficult to envision or is not thought of. The principal difficulty is in the construction of the downhill side below the terrace, because the surface of the pond must of course be at terrace level. It would be ideal if there were enough space there so that the slope would continue gradually below the base of the mound supporting the terrace.

This kind of installation is extraordinarily interesting. When you step out onto the terrace, you look directly at the water's surface with its morning and evening moods and with lighting effects at night created by submerged or surface lights. A stairway leads below the surface of the pool. A spill fountain with gently splashing water in or next to the pool creates an atmosphere of magical solitude—and all of this right next to your seat!

A pool with a flexible liner installed in this way should in no case be overly large, and its dimensions must be in harmony with those of the terrace. It must also be kept in mind that here on the terrace the water produces a considerable amount of internal pressure, which may

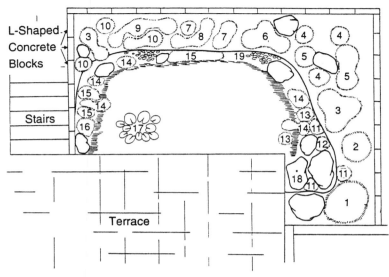

L-Shaped Concrete Blocks

Stairs

Terrace

have to be opposed by a wall set solidly with mortar on the downslope side. With smaller ponds sufficient stability can be achieved with L-shaped concrete blocks, which must be firmly anchored in the ground and strengthened by pebbles mounded up against them. When this supporting construction is later covered with soil and seeded, it will no longer be visible.

Of course, a pre-shaped pool could also be used in place of a flexible liner. If small children are in the home, however, this terrace pool also represents a source of danger which must not be underestimated. It would thus seem advisable to postpone such a fascinating project for a few years. Since it would come under a great deal of traffic, it would be impossible to make it safe without destroying the whole effect.

Ponds with terraces can be dangerous for small children.

THE RAISED POOL

This form is ideal for an enclosed paved courtyard or atrium, and wherever you do not want to or cannot excavate a hole for a pool.

The construction is simple. Two courses of railroad ties or other square timbers are overlapped in a rectangle and the liner is wedged securely between the stacked ties. The center of the liner hangs down from the timbers and rests on a bed of sand. The pool can be filled with soil or the plants set in containers. As an alternative to railroad ties, a framework of natural stone or brick masonry is also possible—depending on which material is best suited for the house and garden.

If the pond rests against a wall or the side of the house, higher aquatic and bog plants, such as bulrush *(Scirpus lacustris)*, yellow flag *(Iris pseudacorus)*, flowering rush *(Butomus umbellatus)*, arrowhead *(Sagittaria sagittifolia)*, or pickerel weed *(Pontederia cordata)*, are placed in the background. If the pool is accessible from all sides, plants of this size are used

more sparingly. At a water's depth of 30 to 40 centimeters (the raised pond does not allow more) an abundant assortment of small-growing plants of the shallow zones up to water lilies and other floating foliage plants are also eligible, like water fringe *(Nymphoides peltata)*, water chestnut *(Trapa natans)*, and water crowfoot *(Ranunculus aquatilis)*.

Very decorative here is a large clump of container-grown umbrella grass *(Cyperus alternifolius)*, which is overwintered indoors in a bright place, or the water hyacinth *(Eichhornia crassipes)* with its light-blue flowers, which

The arrowhead *(Sagittaria sagittifolia)*, a popular shallow-water plant.

also can be cultivated in winter in a bright, warm window. Because the raised pond lacks a margin, potted plants can be placed on the ties or container-grown plants can be set outside them.

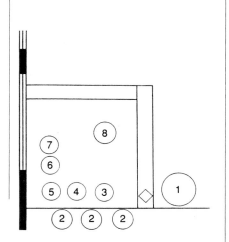

1. angel's trumpet in container (*Brugmansia* or *Datura*); 2. fuchsia in basins; 3. arrowhead (*Sagittaria sagittifolia*); 4. bog iris *(Iris pseudacorus)*; 5. umbrella plant (*Cyperus alternifolius*); 6. pickerel weed (*Pontederia cordata*); 7. golden club *(Orontium aquatica)*; 8. water lily.

1. bog arum *(Calla palustris)*; 2. water forget-me-not *(Myosotis palustris)*; 3. marsh marigold *(Caltha palustris)*; 4. Lake Constance forget-me-not *(Myosotis rehsteineri)*; 5. primula *(Primula)*; 6. cotton grass *(Eriophorum vaginatum)*; 7. cuckoo flower *(Cardamine pratensis)*; 8. globe flower *(Trollius europaeus)*; 9. floating pond weed *(Potamogeton natans)*; 10. water splurge *(Euphorbia palustris)*; 11. dwarf cattail *(Typha minima)*;

THE BOG GARDEN

Usually the adjoining bog garden will already be planned during the construction of the garden pond. It is also possible, however, to install a separate shallow-water pool and to dispense entirely with the pond. Here too there is no limit to the choices, and the possibilities range from a miniature bog in a fairly large household basin placed at ground level to an extensive liner construction.

This pool should be filled with a mixture of peat and, if possible, loamy soil, but there should still be enough room above it for 15 to 20 centimeters of water over it. Otherwise the installation of a bog garden differs little from that of a "proper" pond, except that no submerged, floating foliage plants or fishes can live there.

In return there is an abundance of other plants **(see "Plants for Bogs and Shallow Water," page 61),** which require some water over their roots or at least a moist substrate. Bog bean *(Menyanthes trifoliata),* which opens its white flowers starting in April, is one of the first early bloomers. The bog

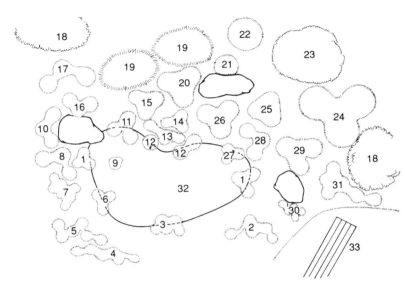

arum *(Calla palustris)* also has white flowers and the cylindrical spadix typical of members of the arum family. Marsh marigold *(Caltha palustris)* and water forget-me-not *(Myosotis palustris)* contribute yellow and blue flowers, whereas purple loosestrife *(Lythrum salicaria)* and Joe-Pye weed *(Eupatorium purpureum)* cover the red part of the spectrum. The pygmy cattail *(Typha minima)*, bur reed *(Sparganium erectum)*, and the morningstar sedge *(Carex grayi)*, with their spiny seed heads, also feel at home in the bog.

In the creation of the margin it should be kept in mind that here, even more so than with a pond, it is a question of trying to imitate a natural wet biotope, whose charm should not be altered by unsuitable materials in the immediate vicinity.

12. brooklime *(Veronica beccabunga)*; 13. morningstar sedge *(Carex grayi)*; 14. bog kidney fern *(Thelypteris palustris)*; 15. Siberian iris *(Iris sibirica)*; 16. meadow sweet *(Filipendula ulmaria)*; 17. daylily *(Hemerocallis)*; 18. red-twigged dogwood *(Cornus sanguinea)*; 19. bamboo; 20. plantain lily *(Hosta)*; 21. royal fern *(Osmunda regalis)*; 22. *Telekia speciosa*; 23. willow *(Salix)*; 24. Joe-Pye weed *(Eupatorium)*; 25. purple loosestrife *(Lythrum salicaria)*; 26. branched bur reed *(Sparganium erectum)*; 27. bog bean *(Menyanthes trifoliata)*; 28. bog iris *(Iris laevigata)*; 29. yellow flag *(Iris pseudacorus)*; 30. checkerboard fritillaria *(Fritillaria meleagris)*; 31. alkanet *(Brunnera macrophylla)*; 32. open water surface; 33. bench.

Adjacent to the bog garden can be a formal pond.

THE NATURAL POND

In contrast to the geometric pond and other artificial kinds of pools, this is an installation that imitates nature and is preferentially called a "wet biotope" by serious biogardeners *(for illustration see opposite page).* You should not set such narrow limits, however, that the enjoyment of your own garden is lost. When a flexible liner is used, there is a wide range of choices in the design, and the shape and size can be adapted to existing conditions.

More so than in other gardens, the background, marginal, and pond plantings are in the forefront. Hybrid roses and fancy perennials are just as

out of place in the vicinity of a natural body of water as Colorado blue spruces or formal hedges. Wherever possible, native shrubs like hazel, wild plum, or sea buckthorn should be used, and for the marginal area wild perennials, like those offered today in a wide assortment by any perennial nursery *(see "Plants for the Marginal Zone," page 64).* An extensive shallow-water zone is important, which permits the enlargement of the available plant material for bog plants and offers a home to numerous insects that live in and on the water. Where there is insufficient room for this kind of biotope, at the very least there should be an adjoining bog garden, which can get by with little space. A few large rocks, a rootstock, or a gnarled branch assume decorative functions and replace stone statues and other ornaments.

Unnecessary meddling into the natural pond should be avoided. The plants should be left to themselves as long as possible, and cautious intervention is called for only when the wild growth obscures the view of the water.

Facing page: the natural pond.

THE STREAM

The stream need not necessarily be joined to an existing pond, but can rather be integrated into the garden as an independent design element. Its water, which ripples quietly over stones and perhaps comes almost to a standstill in small bays or quickens its movement over a miniature dam, creates together with the marginal planting a very special kind of mood. *(see illustration page 25).*

Neither a wide stream bed nor extensive excavation work are necessary. The only requirement is a gentle slope, which need not be greater than two centimeters per running meter, and therefore can also be created in any garden by building up a low stream bed.

Where the size of the garden permits, the stream should be allowed to flow in a gentle bend, or the water should be diverted here and there with large rocks in the marginal area so that a natural effect is produced. Through constant evaporation there is a noticeable increase in the humidity around the running water from which the plants that grow here profit. They also find a place to their liking in the moist zone of the bank. For example, blue, white, and red-blossomed bugle *(Ajuga reptans)*, which prefers somewhat shaded sites, cuckoo flower *(Cardamine pratensis)*, with its delicate lilac blossoms, and in yellow and blue the iris species *Iris forrestii, Iris wilsonii,* and *Iris chrysographes.* Even ferns, such as the two-meter-high royal fern *(Osmunda regalis)* or the delicate lady fern *(Athyrium filix-femina)*, feel at home in the humid air along the edge of the stream.

For the early spring flowering, small bulbs, such as snowdrop, winter aconite, or bluebell *(Scilla)*, can be planted and naturalized here. The role of shrubs can be taken over by tall perennials, such as garden spirea *(Astilbe)*.

Facing page: the stream.

SPRING STONES

This is the simplest and most space-saving way to introduce water into the garden—it is even possible on a balcony, roof-top garden or terrace! Complete sets with a spring stone, small pump, and catch basin are offered in garden centers, which come ready to install in the garden or on the terrace.

Somewhat more expensive are millstones or granite blocks with a hole bored in them to conduct water, that can be used to create tranquil places, perhaps in the half shade of trees or bushes.

The spring stone can, for example, be set on a bed of gravel, which will be dampened by the trickling water and give off cool dampness on hot summer days.

In strict geometric gardens, the fountain fits in the middle of a surface with flagstones or artificial stones. In the natural garden a large boulder would probably be more appropriate. In this case, however, a stone mason with a suitable tool must bore the hole.

The spring stone can also be integrated into an existing pond, either on a raised pedestal directly in the water or outside in a suitable place. It can also be used as the starting point for a stream. Surprising effects can be achieved with this kind of installation wherever water in motion is not expected, such as on the lawn or in the courtyard of a paved atrium. The planting is determined by the type of spring and its surroundings. Where there is no area of open water, plants that prefer moist soils can be planted at the edge of the gravel bed: creeping Jenny (Lysimachia nummularia), which soon carpets the stones with its green-leaved creeping shoots, or for flowering plants musk (Mimulus luteus), water forget-me-not (Myosotis palustris), or globe flower (Trollius europaeus).

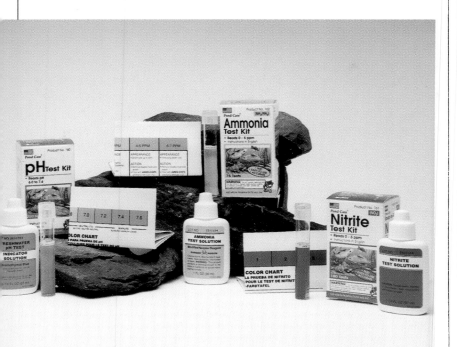

Testing of the water destined for use in garden pools and ponds for its ammonia and nitrite levels as well as for its pH and hardness has been made much easier for hobbyists because of the introduction of test kits that are reliable and easy to use. Photo courtesy of Aquarium Pharmaceuticals.

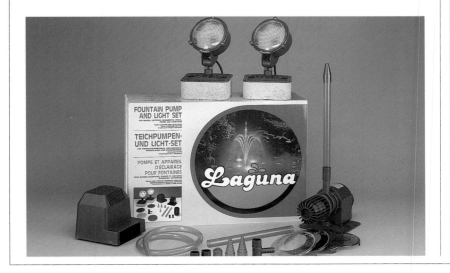

Left: Sets that include both fountain and lights for aquatic pools are available at pet shops. Photo courtesy of Rolf C. Hagen Corp.

FOUNTAINS AND SPLASH SCULPTURE

Anyone who is considering a water fountain, splash sculpture, and the like must realize that this kind of constant spraying is not tolerated by plants and animals. The only exception is when a ring is used below the fountain so that the surrounding water's surface is barely stirred. This sort of arrangement is even accepted by water lilies, which are particularly sensitive to moving water as long as they grow some distance away *(for illustration see page 30)*.

The retail market offers special fountain pumps of different sizes with appropriate spray heads and a variety of jets, which are adjustable in some cases so that the spray can be regulated.

A fountain of this kind certainly has its charm (in an appropriate setting), especially when interesting effects at night are achieved through the use of supplemental lighting, including submerged fixtures. On the other hand, you should also consider that the constant sound of falling water is not to everyone's taste and under certain circumstances you should choose a gentler spray. Large fountains, such as are found in public installations, are in any case hardly suitable for the home garden.

More modest is splash sculpture in the form of figures, which are suitable for many pools as ornamental and decorative elements. Stone or ceramic fishes; wading birds in copper, which over time develop a shimmering green patina; amphibians, such as frogs or salamanders; and many more too numerous to mention here are available.

Facing page: A natural pond with fountains and splash sculpture.

Filters and water pumps designed for use in garden pools come in a number of different sizes and levels of power to fit pools of varying sizes and depths. Photo courtesy of E.G. Danner.

Above: A hole drilled through the boulder converts it to a splash stone.

Facing page: The two photos show simple miniature water gardens created from wooden barrels cut in half (top) and a more formal miniature garden with stones and a plastic liner to make it waterproof (below).

Of course, many are also marketed in plastic today.

Tasteful plastic objects of this kind also fit well into a pond with natural-appearing structures like large stones, old tree roots, and bamboo or Japanese maples as a backdrop. In case of doubt it is best not to use them as functional fountains at all, but instead to let them act as decorative elements.

MINIATURE WATER GARDEN

Depending on the size of the terrace or balcony, various ideas are possible. The simplest form is a fairly large container, which should be wide rather than high. Particularly attractive are wooden barrels cut in half, such as are offered in garden centers as planters *(for illustration see facing page).* But any other kind of container is also suitable (if it is attractive and fits in with the surroundings), since with the aid of liners it is no longer a problem to make it waterproof today.

A water depth of only 20 centimeters is deep enough for a dwarf water lily, a dwarf cattail *(Typha minima),* or a small umbrella grass *(Cyperus),* which can winter in a

bright place in the house. It is essential, however, to avoid overstocking the container with plants.

Also avoid a site exposed to full sun. The water would heat up so much that no plant could survive in it for long.

Where no natural shade is present, a suitable device must be installed, such as cloth or screening material stretched on a wooden frame. This is set up in the direction of the sun and can be moved if necessary.

This kind of miniature pond will have to be moved to a bright place in the house when it is in danger of freezing all the way to the bottom. Or it can be packed in styrofoam and burlap *(also see page 49)* so that it can be wintered outdoors.

Somewhat more expensive, but also more attractive, is a pre-shaped pool, which is installed at ground level in the soil on the terrace. This is then already a proper water garden, which of course also offers more latitude in regard to the planting. Depending upon the structure of one's terrace, one can remove some flagstones, adding additional soil space for planting, which need not be in any way inferior to the arrangement of a garden pond. As with the previously described pool on a terrace slope, the necessary safety measures must be followed here, particularly when small children play on the terrace without supervision.

There is almost no waterproof container which is unsuitable for a water garden. This old 50 gallon aluminum pot worked very well on a terrace.

Practical Water Gardening

Of all the parts of the home garden, the intact garden pond requires the least care. And not only that; it is best to intervene as little as possible, and yet also not to leave the pond completely to its own devices. But what has to be done in the summer is usually only a matter of small corrections or slight retouching, such as the transplanting of a plant or two, pruning branches that overhang too much, or removing an occasional dead water-lily leaf.

The marginal area, that consists of a flower bed or a perennial border, requires somewhat more care, but really requires the same maintenance as anywhere else: watering in times of dryness, hoeing the soil, weeding, thinning and transplanting, and occasionally working in compost or an organic commercial fertilizer to replenish the nutrient reserves. To make sure the pond quickly finds its biological balance, a few fundamental principles should be kept in mind at the time of installation.

THE POND TAKES SHAPE

The preparatory work, such as the excavation of the hole, the leveling of the substrate, and the installation of a liner or a pre-shaped pool, will not be discussed further here.

We assume that all of the preparatory work was done correctly, and will begin with the objective to fill the construction with life. These are, above all, the plants which are to have

The planted bank. It begins about 40 centimeters below the water's surface and rises gradually to the pond margin. The planting substrate is covered with sand or gravel. Invasive plants, such as cattails (Typha), must be planted in a container.

In the creation of the bank make sure that tall plants are planted in the background, and low ones in the foreground. In this way the water's surface remains visible.

their place here, and for which conditions suitable for growth must first be created.

THE RIGHT SUBSTRATE

Even when you decide not to let your aquatic plants root freely, but rather to cultivate them exclusively in wire baskets, the bottom of the pool should have a shallow covering of sand or gravel or both. This substrate provides stability for the plant containers. It is also beneficial for the

innumerable micro-organisms that soon become established and help to transform organic substances into nutrients for the plants. This lightly colored layer is present for only a short time and is soon covered by deposits, which produce a gradually growing film of fine mulm.

If all or some of the plants are to be planted directly, the bottom of the pond must be filled with a growth medium. It need not be deeper than 15 to 20 centimeters, because with very few excep-

40 cm · 20 cm · 30 cm · 40 cm

tions the aquatic plants have shallow root systems. Furthermore, they take up a part of their nutrients not only from the substrate, but also directly from the water by means of the finest of rootlets. Loamy or sandy soil, which should be as low in nutrients as possible and free of chemical fertilizers, is suitable as a substrate. If soil from the garden is used, it should be taken from deeper layers, which as a rule are largely free of nutrients and fertilizer residues. On the other hand, the uppermost layer of topsoil of the cultivated garden is not only nutrient-rich, but also contains many organic components that are in a state of decomposition, which will produce cloudiness and the formation of methane gas in the pond. For this same

Typha, one of the invasive plants best kept segregated in a container.

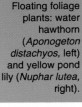

Floating foliage plants: water hawthorn (*Aponogeton distachyos*, left) and yellow pond lily (*Nuphar lutea*, right).

reason garden compost is also unsuitable as a substrate for aquatic plants.

To prevent suspended matter from being stirred up, it is best to cover the substrate with a thin layer of sand or gravel. If containers or wire baskets are used, the same rules apply to filling them.

THE RIGHT WATER

Anyone who builds a garden pond for the first time must face the problem of the water quality. One of the most commonly asked questions is: Should rain water or tap water be used? In communities with heavy air pollution, rain water is not always the most suitable medium, and even in less polluted places the rain should be allowed to run off the roof for a while before it is collected for filling the pond.

It is easier to use water straight from the tap. This water is ideal at first, but within a short time the chlorine will evaporate and the water will be colonized by living organisms.

It does not injure plants if they are initially placed in water of this kind, but

you should wait a few weeks before introducing fishes, because they are more sensitive to the water than plants.

FILLING WITH WATER

Regardless of what you fill your pond with, the water should enter gently and slowly. A strong spray from the hose not only stirs up the substrate, it also uproots the plants or at least loosens them; one day they will be floating on the surface, and it will take some effort to put the roots back where they belong. The simplest and most practical solution is to place the end of the hose in a bucket standing in the pond (preferably tied to the handle) and to allow the water to flow over the side. Another method is to tie a sack over the end of the hose to diffuse the flow of water.

Plants for shallow water (water depth of about 30 centimeters): bog bean (*Menyanthes trifoliata*, left) and pickerel weed (*Pontederia cordata*, right).

Facing page: (top): Plants for shallow water (water depth of about five centimeters): yellow flag (*Iris pseudacorus*, left) and flowering rush (*Butomus umbellatus*, right).

(right): Water lilies and other floating foliage leaves are best set on a mound on the bottom of the pond. It consists of a small pile of planting medium (ten centimeters high with a diameter of 50 centimeters), which is covered with a 10-to-15-centimeter-thick layer of gravel. The mound can have a diameter of more than one meter, so that it does not float up to the surface after a few years. Safe wintering is possible with a water depth of 70 centimeters or more.

Facing page: (bottom): Plants for the bog: purple loosestrife (*Lythrum salicaria*, left) and Siberian iris (*Iris sibirica*, right).

THE PLANTS IN THE POND

The supply and assortment of plants for the pool is greatest in May when nurseries, garden centers, and supermarkets with garden departments have been freshly supplied. When aquatic and bog plants are purchased in the spring, you should not be

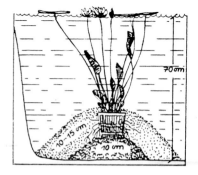

influenced too much by their initially homely or stunted appearance. Usually they have only just begun to grow after the winter dormancy, and the young greenery has a hard time forcing its way through the heavy, old shoots and remains of leaves that are still attached. You should therefore not expect to find specimens at this time that resemble those shown in catalogs, books, or magazines. The growth that will soon begin at home in the pond will then demonstrate all the more the energy and vitality that aquatic plants contain.

PLANTING DIRECTLY OR IN CONTAINERS?

The method that is decided on depends largely on the size of the installation. Because many pond plants are invasive and their roots wander freely in or on the substrate and produce more and more new shoots, container plantings are preferable in the small pond. A particularly drastic example of unlimited invasiveness is given by the spire reed *(Phragmites australis)*. This 1.80 meter-high grass can only be restricted to the margin of the pond when it is confined by a barrier in the substrate, and even then should only be used in larger bodies of water.

With water lilies opinion differs as to whether they should be planted directly in the substrate or are better grown in containers. Freely growing water lilies can, in the course of time, cover a whole pond with their foliage, so that one day it will be necessary to take out and divide the rhizomes. This is hard work, by the way, because the large rootstocks are usually anchored firmly in the substrate and can be loosened only with difficulty.

In practice, container planting has proved to be the best solution, at least

in modestly constructed water gardens, without the blossoms being impaired substantially by the container. Plants in movable containers can also be transplanted easily when the planting is changed or increased.

SHOULD YOU FERTILIZE?

Plants rooted directly in the substrate require no fertilizers. The water itself and the substrate supply sufficient nutrients, which are constantly replenished by dead plant parts and small animals (or fish waste products). The same is true of container plants, to which only water lilies can be an exception. A reduction in flowers and small leaves are symptoms of nutrient deficiency, which indicates that a supplemental fertilization is necessary. Because as little fertilizer as possible should dissolve into the water during application, only the soil in the plant container should be supplied with fertilizer.

If the container can be lifted out, bone meal or a chemical fertilizer should be pressed as deeply as possible into the substrate. If the container must stay in the water, fertilizer spikes can be used. Another possibility is to knead the fertilizer into little balls of loam or mix it into a paste with water, and then to permit these mixtures to dry out. Once in a dry/solid form, they can be inserted into the vicinity of the roots.

ANIMALS BY AND IN THE WATER

It is amazing what power of attraction water has on animals of the most diverse kinds and how little time it takes before this becomes apparent. As soon as the vegetation opens out in the pond and the days grow warmer, the first guests check in; visitors the likes of which have never been seen in the garden before and which we do not necessarily associate with water. Among these are insects, of which butterflies and dragonflies are the most conspicuous. If bushes grow near the

Frogs often manage to invade garden ponds if there is a nearby natural body of water that houses them. Photo of by Michael Gilroy.

pond, birds will soon appear—chickadees, sparrows, blackbirds, and of course the ubiquitous robins, which like to bathe in the shallow water.

Bullfrogs and green frogs also find their way all by themselves, if there is a natural body of water anywhere in the immediate vicinity or further afield. Treefrogs, which visit the water only to breed in early spring and like their amphibious relatives perform small concerts, are usually discovered when mowing the lawn in the morning or toward evening. Nocturnal toads, on the other hand, lead such secretive lives that they are encountered only by accident, such as on a garden path after dark or even on the terrace.

Insectivorous shrews also like to take up quarters in the vicinity of a pond. That garter snakes, mice, and rabbits also find their way to a densely grown garden pond probably has less to do with the water than with the piles of leaves and rocks, old tree trunks, and hiding places.

By far the greatest diversity in species, however, is found in the pond itself, although you have to look closely to detect the life there. Water snails are easy enough to see as they peacefully graze algae from plants and rocks. The waterstriders and whirligig beetles that flit about on the water's surface are also impossible to overlook. Water spiders, crustaceans, water

If fishes are present in the pond and amphibians such as salamanders or frogs are also desired, a spawning pond can be constructed. This is located in the marginal area of the pond and is separated from it by a pile of coarse gravel. In this way the water can flow into the spawning pond, but the fishes cannot pass through the barrier.

There is no compelling reason for having fish in your water garden, but many people would not think of a water garden without colorful, tame fish like the koi (Japanese colored carp) shown here.

bugs, and the most diverse insect larvae require some effort to detect. Also hard to find is the predaceous diving beetle, which only comes to the surface to get air and at almost four centimeters long is our largest native aquatic beetle. Like its larvae, it preys on, among other things, tadpoles and other small aquatic creatures which scarcely stand out from the dark bottom of the pond.

FISHES: A TOUGH CHOICE

There is no compelling reason to stock a garden pond with fishes. Some things even speak against doing so; for some species of fishes can threaten the plants or wipe out the small-animal fauna (a way to maintain amphibians in the water without the fishes disturbing them is represented by the spawning pool—see accompanying illustration). Of paramount importance in the pros and cons is the size of the installation. In a small pond you should be more cautious in stocking fishes or avoid doing so altogether. In larger bodies of water, small koi, bitterlings, or minnows can scarcely cause damage. And what of the goldfish, the champion among the finned pond inhabitants? Here the opinions are strongly divided.

These descendants of the

Asian silver carp are not highly valued by serious garden pond keepers. For them, if at all, only native species are suitable. But even less committed gardeners balk at buying because it is generally claimed that the goldfish through its grubbing causes permanent clouding of the water, and as a voracious feeder correspondingly produces a lot of excrement, therefore contributing to the growth of algae.

But contrary experiences also exist. Many pond owners have kept goldfish for years without having observed any detrimental effects at all. Even their high reproductive rate, occasionally mentioned as a negative, is self-regulating. As an educational tool, it is fun, particularly for children, to observe the growth of such specimens, and to see how plain gray or black juveniles develop into ornately colored goldfish. This also awakens their interest in the other small or large inhabitants of the biotope in their own garden.

THINGS THAT CAN SPOIL THE PLEASURE: ALGAE AND PESTS

Algae, and in particular

In any pond situation, be sure the edges of the pond are shallow enough to prevent accidental drowning should a small child fall into the water.

the tiny free-floating algae, are the nightmare of every pond owner. Once they appear, the water will never be clear, and its cloudiness is also discouraging. Misfortune of this kind happens again and again, particularly in a newly installed pond in which the interplay of the various elements—from the substrate to the fishes to the plants—is not yet coordinated and in balance.

Whether free-floating or the initially less damaging filamentous algae, their presence always points to the overloading of the water with organic substances, that is plant food. To put it more simply: if the fertilizer in the water and the substrate cannot be taken up and processed by the plants in the pond, the excess is available as food for the algae and promotes their sometimes explosive growth.

This is also the reason why neither chemical nor organic fertilizers, such as the frequently recommended cow manure or compost for water lilies, have any business in the garden pond. The same algae-promoting effect is achieved through the uncontrolled feeding of the fishes, which simultaneously causes two undesirable effects. On the one hand, uneaten food sinks to the bottom where it decomposes and produces an excess of nutrients. On the other, the more that is fed, the more fish excrement will be produced.

When faced with a persistent growth of algae, the beginner usually takes radical measures as the seemingly most suitable response. In the hopes of eradicating the pest lock, stock, and barrel, he performs a complete water

Pet shops usually carry a wide range of foods for pond fishes and other pool inhabitants. Photo courtesy of Wardley.

change. In this way, to be sure, he temporarily gets rid of the suspended algae, but simultaneously destroys all of the small animals and microorganisms which have just become established in the water. Because algae spores also arrive through the air and are still present in the empty pond, the misery starts up again after a while.

MEASURES AGAINST FILAMENTOUS ALGAE

In the small pond, life can be made difficult for filamentous algae by acidifying the water with a sack of peat or a bunch of straw hung in the water. The algae can also be pulled out by hand or with a rake (caution with pool liners). Also, by removing their food supply, they will no longer have a chance to survive and should disappear without a trace.

The following should be done:

* In the event that the pond's substrate was fertilized, not much can be done. In this case you must live with the algae until the fertilizer has been used up.
* Reduce the feeding of the fishes immediately.
* If a large number of fishes have been introduced, reduce the population.

* Establish submerged plants; they not only take in nutrients through the roots, but with the foliage as well. To these useful plants, which in part send their leaves to the water's surface, belong starwort *(Callitriche palustris)*, hornwort *(Ceratophyllum demersum)*, hydrilla *(Hydrilla verticillata)*, whorled milfoil *(Myriophyllum verticillatum)*, and spreading crowfoot *(Ranunculus circinatus)*. Chemical remedies should never be used in the garden pond, even if this has been recommended at

These submerged plants can help when algae are a problem (from left to right): hornwort, whorled milfoil, water crowfoot, and starwort.

times and is also practiced with success by well-versed commercial gardeners. With improper use everything can be ruined in this way, and it will be a long time before you will get a handle on a water garden following such a radical cure.

The same applies to insecticides (to control pests) and fungicides (to control fungi), which should be avoided in the garden in general and particularly in the pond! All pyrethrum-based insecticides, for example, are highly toxic to fishes, yet they have occasionally even been recommended by biogardeners because they are not dangerous to warm-blooded animals.

ANIMAL PESTS

Thankfully animal pests are not found too frequently in the pond, but of course water lilies and other aquatic plants are not immune to various insects like aphids. Spraying them off with a stream of water is not very effective, because the aphids are equipped with a layer of wax and will survive the involuntary bath without injury until they can cling to the nearest plant and climb up. If the threatened specimens are within reach, heavily infested parts are cut off and put on the compost pile or the aphids are crushed with the fingers. If they are farther away, long-handled pruners, such as are used for trimming tree branches at great heights, have proved effective.

The same methods are also used against the leaf-eating larvae of the waterlily beetle and the caterpillars of the brown China mark moth.

WHEN THE POND "CLOSES OVER"

This can happen faster than you would believe at first, particularly in small pools. Not only can water lilies rapidly cover an entire body of water with their large leaves, but other floating foliage plants like the yellow pond lily (Nuphar lutea) or floating pond weed (Potamogeton natans) also have this trait and must be thinned occasionally. In this case the leaves should be cut off as far below the water's surface as possible. When even this is not effective, with water lilies and yellow pond lilies the rhizome will have to be reduced in size.

Branched bur reed (Sparganium erectum), morningstar sedge (Carex grayi), and cattail species (Typha) spread invasively if they are not planted in containers. Pruning or pulling up plants will occasionally be necessary to prevent the plants from completely taking over, obstructing the view of the open water. In addition, purple loosestrife *(Lythrum salicaria)*, water plantain *(Alisma plantago-aquatica)*, and yellow musk *(Mimulus luteus)* can become pests through self-perpetuation. Because it is not likely that anyone will want to deprive themselves of the flowers by preventing the formation of seeds, only the rigorous removal of all excess specimens is advised.

What was already mentioned previously, however, also applies here. Whenever possible the garden pond, whether large or small, should be left to its own devices. The aforementioned actions should always be viewed as emergency measures and never the rule.

THE POND IN FALL AND WINTER

When the nights grow colder, the activity of the pond and its surroundings also starts to wind down. Insects and fishes withdraw into deeper water, butterflies and dragonflies have long since disappeared, and even the birds

Fresh leaves and fresh flower petals create severe oxygen-robbing litter. In the pond they sink to the bottom and through their composition the oxygen content of the water can drop drastically.

visit the water only occasionally for a late bath. These fall days offer the opportunity to bring some order to the water garden and, if necessary, clean up from the neglect of summer.

SOME CLEANING IS NECESSARY

So that methane gas does not form under the covering of ice in the winter, all of the plant parts that are no longer bright green and healthy are removed from the water during the fall.

The removal of dead leaves should also occur at this time at the latest. Likewise, submerged plants growing luxuriantly can be thinned out and invasive sedges or rushes can be pulled. On the other hand, planting must wait for spring or early summer.

If deciduous trees or shrubs stand near the pond, it could prove to be advantageous to cover the pond's surface with bird netting to protect from falling leaves. The netting catches the leaves, and as soon as the trees are bare it is carefully pulled from the pond with its contents. With smaller ponds it is sufficient to skim the leaves from time to time with the aid of a fishing net.

WHAT ABOUT WINTER PROTECTION?

Assuming that only winter-hardy plants and fishes inhabit the pond and that it is at least 60 centimeters deep in one place, no preventive measures need be made for the winter. All life adapts to the lowered water temperatures and in a manner of speaking continues to run on "pilot light." As soon as a thick layer of ice capable of supporting your weight has formed, you can use the opportunity to cut back or thin out shrubs that stand close by the pond, which otherwise are hard to get at.

On the other hand, this solid covering of ice is the only thing that can be dangerous in winter, especially to fishes. It primarily prevents gas exchange, that is, oxygen cannot enter the water and methane gas cannot escape. If there are tall-growing plants, such as reeds, cattails, rushes (Juncus), or purple loosestrife, the dry stalks or shoots should be left standing above the water. They develop so much heat as they decompose that tiny air canals develop in the ice, through which the gases can pass. As a substitute, bundles of straw or twigs can be placed in the water before the first hard frost. This will have the same effect.

Evergreen submerged

plants, such as Canadian potweed *(Elodea canadensis)* or shining pondweed *(Potamogeton lucens),* remain active during the cold season and act as suppliers of oxygen under the covering of ice.

If no plants are available as helpers, pieces of styrofoam, which can be broken off packaging material, will do the same thing. In addition, plastic pool covers, which keep the water free of ice, are available in garden centers. Electric pond heaters also exist, but they are for keeping the water's surface free of ice, not for general heating. Probably simpler is an air pump, which can be connected somewhere near the house and equipped with a pencil-thin hose that reaches to the pond. The expelled air not only prevents ice formation by agitating the water's surface, but simultaneously enriches the water with oxygen.

THE SPECIAL CASE OF MINIATURE WATER GARDENS

Since it is usually a question here of relatively small and shallow containers, it cannot be ruled out that the pool may freeze solid during long periods of intense cold. If the miniature pond is transportable, it should be brought into a cool, bright

room in the house in extremely cold weather. It should, however, be brought in as late as possible and put back outside as soon as possible.

If it is impossible to move the pool, the basin should be wrapped with leaves, styrofoam, peat, or some other insulating material before covering it with bubble wrap and protecting it from snow drifts. The water level should be lowered by about ten centimeters and sheets of styrofoam or bubble wrap placed on the water's surface.

To winter a miniature water garden on the balcony or terrace, on the north, east, and possibly on the west side an insulating layer of styrofoam (five to eight centimeters) is attached. Finally the whole miniature water garden is packed in bubble wrap (it must not rest on the water), in which holes are out for large plants. It is important that the sun reaches the south and top side, so that the water is continually warmed slightly.

Plants for the Garden Pond

The frogbit *(Hydrocharis morsus-ranae)*.

Floating Foliage Plants

These are plants that are usually equipped with a system of fine roots, which takes up nutrients directly from the water or the substrate. Thus, the floating plant willow grass *(Polygonum amphibium)* forms runners. This category with fluid transitional forms includes direct-rooting genera, such as water lilies or water hyacinth, which have leaves that float on the water's surface. Because many species propagate rapidly and can cover large parts of the pond with their floating leaves (well-fertilized, luxuriantly growing water lilies come to mind), it is important to keep an eye on them and to occasionally thin them out, as is the case with the duckweed *(Lemna minor)*. At first the green islands of tiny leaves look attractive and the surface is brightened, but when the ever-growing carpets join, a portion of them should be removed.

No one knows exactly what the floating plant frogbit *(Hydrocharis morsus-ranae)* has to do with frogs. The six-centimeter-wide leaves, which are sent to the surface from the winter buds that winter on the bottom of the pond, adorn themselves in July and August with small white flowers with a yellow spot at the base of each petal. Frogbit is not overly attractive, but does resemble water-lily leaves in miniature format and provides variety in parts of the water where vegetation is absent. The yearly regeneration of this plant

can only be expected in installations with a natural substrate for the wintering of the winter buds.

The flower of the water hawthorn *(Aponogeton distachyos)* gives off a strong scent of vanilla **(illustrated on page 36).**

The water chestnut *(Trapa natans)*, on the other hand, must be purchased anew each spring, because it is an annual plant; its fruits cannot ripen in our climate. Particularly charming with this plant is the dark red fall coloration of the rosettes of its floating, toothed, rhomboidal leaves. This and the majority of the species listed in the table **(see below)** have a water-cleansing and algae-inhibiting effect, because they remove nutrients from the pond with their roots or leaves. Therefore, despite their tendency to become invasive, they should be allowed to establish themselves in your water garden and only the excess should be removed. Furthermore, ecologically speaking, it is just as worthwhile to strive for a diversity of plants in the pond as on land, as long as the organizing hand of the gardener intervenes at the right time.

WATER LILIES

The water lilies of the genus *Nymphaea* number among the largest and most beautiful flowering plants of the garden pond. The family of the water lilies (Nymphaeaceae) includes a total of eight genera and about 65 species, of which 40 are water lilies and two are lotuses *(Nelumbo)*.

The most astonishing water lily, which can only be admired in the exhibits of botanical gardens, is the

FLOATING FOLIAGE PLANTS				
Botanical Name	Common Name	Water Depth in cm	Flower Color	Flowering Period
Aponogeton distachyos	water hawthorn	40-80	white	June to September
Eichhornia crassipes	water hyacinth	-	blue-violet	to September
Hydrocharis morsus-ranae	frogbit	20-40	white	June to August
Lemna minor	duckweed	at least 1	none	none
Nuphar lutea	yellow pond lily	40-200	yellow	June to September
Nymphoides peltata	water fringe	20-50	yellow	July to August
Polygonum amphibium	willow grass	30-60	pink	June to August
Potamogeton natans	floating pondweed	30-100	white	June to August
Ranunculus aquatilis	water crowfoot	20-50	white	June to August
Stratiotes aloides	water soldier	40-100	white	June to August
Trapa natans	water chestnut	40-120	white	June to September

Water lilies and other plants are planted in wire planting baskets. From left to right: A planting basket is lined with newspaper. After filling the basket with the planting substrate the plant is put in and covered with sand (two centimeters). After thorough watering the protruding newspaper is torn off at the edge of the basket. The newspaper disintegrates in the water and the plants can send their roots through the basket. Therefore, use only paper.

giant water lily *Victoria amazonica* (formerly *Victoria regia*). With respect to flowers and leaves it is among the giants of the plant world. It is worthwhile to become better acquainted with it while we look at the starlike flowers of our water lilies floating on the water of the garden pond. *Victoria amazonica* is native to the still bodies of water of the Amazon Basin, where it was discovered in 1801. Its round floating leaves with upward-curled margins attain a diameter of 2.1 meters. The night-flowering, white to pink blossoms are up to 36 centimeters in size, and the rootstock has a thickness of 20 centimeters. Thanks to the thick-ribbed network of veins on the underside, which provides buoyancy, the leaves can carry a weight of up to 75 kilograms. Doubtless a truly impressive relative of our water lilies.

DWARF WATER LILIES

In contrast to the giant water lilies, there are miniature water lilies with flowers measuring only four centimeters in diameter, such as the dwarfs *Nymphaea pygmaea* "Alba" or *Nymphaea tetragona*. In contrast to *Victoria amazonica*, these small forms are easily attainable and make charming inhabitants of basins, tubs, and small pools, where they are more than satisfied with a water depth of only 20 centimeters.

So you do not have to do without water lilies— even if there is no pond in the garden.

A LARGE SELECTION OF VARIETIES

If a pond is present, whether large or small, a large variety of cultivated forms in a wide range of colors is available, such as bright or

creamy white mixed with pink, red, or yellow. Only the hardy, blue-blossomed water lily is not meant to be kept in temperate garden ponds. This color is reserved for more tropically oriented ponds.

Yet the varieties that survive in our climate are enough. "Atropurpurea" with flat, particularly dark red 18-centimeter-wide flowers, has bright yellow stamens in the middle. "Marliacea Chromatella," an old and trusted variety from 1887, which still numbers among the most frequently sold varieties, has 15-centimeter-wide, bright-yellow blossoms. The "Sioux," an old Marliac variety which came on the market in 1908, can even change its color. The flowers are pale yellow at first, then deep orange, before finally turning copper-colored. And in which color group should water gardeners classify the rarely offered "Rote Alpina"? This variety alters its coloration to match the weather. If the weather is cool, the flowers are white to pink; when nice, warm days arrive, they turn bright

red. But like the other water lilies, they only do this from late morning to early evening and then close their blossoms.

Shaded ponds are no place for water lilies. In order for them to bloom prolifically, they need sun and still water.

This point must be considered with the marginal plantings of trees and shrubs or other plants. The gardener should forget about installing a spring or splash fountain in the immediate vicinity of *Nymphaea*.

For wintering, water lilies are removed from garden ponds that are not safe from freezing and brought into a frostfree room. The leaves are cut off below the water's surface and the planting basket is removed.

Dwarf Water Lilies for Water Depths of 20-40 Centimeters:

Name	Flower Color
Nymphaea "Ellisiana"	dark red
N. "Laydeckeri Fulgens"	ruby
N. "Laydeckeri Lilacea"	pink
N. "Laydeckeri Purpurata"	carmine
N. "Princess Elizabeth"	pink
N. pygmaea "Alba"	white
N. pygmaea "Helvola"	pale yellow
N. tetragona	white

Water Lilies for Water Depths of 40-60 Centimeters:

Name	Flower Color
Nymphaea alba "Minor"	pure white
N. "Anna Epple"	pink
N. "Atropurpurea"	dark carmine
N. "Aurora"	orange-dark red
N. "Candidissima Rosea"	pink
N. "Chrysantha"	apricot
N. "Comanche"	orange
N. "Froebelii"	carmine
N. "Gloriosa"	cherry red
N. "Graziella"	reddish orange
N. "Indiana"	copper orange
N. "James Brydon"	cherry red
N. "Mme. Laydecker"	cherry red
N. "Mme. Wilfron Gonnére"	pure pink
N. "Masaniello"	pinkish red
N. "Moorei"	yellow
N. "Newton"	cinnabar
N. odorata "Minor"	pale pink
N. odorata "Rosennymphe"	bright pink
N. odorata "W.B. Shaw"	pale pink
N. "Paul Hariot"	yellow with copper
N. "Pink Opal"	dark pink
N. "Rose Arey"	salmon pink
N. tuberosa "Rosea"	salmon pink
N. "William Faulkner"	ruby

Water Lilies for Water Depths of 60-80 Centimeters:

Name	Flower Color
Nymphaea alba	pure white
N. "Albatros"	pinkish white
N. "Amabilis"	pink
N. "Attraction"	garnet
N. "Cardinal"	red
N. "Charles de Meurville"	wine red
N. "Colonel Welch"	yellow
N. "Conqueror"	dark wine red
N. "Escarboucle"	ruby red
N. "Formosa"	bright pink
N. "Hermine"	pure white
N. "Marliacea Albida"	pure white
N. "Marliacea Carnea"	pinkish white
N. "Marliacea Chromatella"	bright yellow
N. "Marliacea Rosea"	pale pink
N. "Mrs. Richmond"	carmine-pink
N. odorata "Maxima"	pure white
N. odorata "Sulphurea Grandiflora"	sulfur yellow
N. "René Gérard"	carmine
N. "Sanguinea"	carmine
N. "Sioux"	copper yellow/orange
N. "Sunrise"	sulfur yellow
N. tuberosa "Gladstoniana"	pure white
N. tuberosa "Postlingberg"	pure white
N. tuberosa "Richardsonii"	pure white

Water lilies can be planted at various depths. When they cover almost the entire top of the pond they inhibit overheating of the water thus slowing evaporation and algae growth.

SUBMERGED PLANTS

To keep the water clean and to inhibit the formation of algae, submerged plants are almost indispensable in the garden pond—unless you have a pool without animal and plant life, which has been designed specifically for the decorative play of water. The species of this group live either completely or for the most part under water, produce oxygen through photosynthesis, and reduce the nutrient supply for algae. In the majority of species only the flowers find their way above the water's surface. Some also send small leaves upward. A few other species take root in the substrate, and others move here and there without taking a firm hold.

Finally, young fishes often find refuge in the thick tangle of leaves and shoots and sexually mature animals find places to lay their eggs. Because of the masses of microorganisms that live on the plants, in a manner of speaking the food swims right into the mouths of the fish fry.

The water violet (*Hottonia palustris*) belongs to the primrose family (Primulaceae) and opens its white blossoms tinged with pale pink between May and July. After pollination they sink into the water to form seeds. This flowering will not be experienced too often, for the plant demands a clear, nutrient-poor and algae-free living space.

The hornwort (*Ceratophyllum demersum*) travels with its needle-like leaves completely rootless through its element, takes up excess nutrients, and releases substances that apparently have a noxious effect on free-floating algae.

SUBMERGED PLANTS

Botanical Name	Common Name	Water Depth in cm	Flower Color	Flowering Period
Callitriche palustris	starwort	20-60	-	-
Ceratophyllum demersum	hornwort	50-100	-	-
Elodea canadensis	Canadian potweed	10-50	white	May to August
Hottonia palustris	water violet	30-60	pink	May to June
Hydrilla verticillata	hydrilla	30-100	-	-
Myriophyllum spicatum	spiked milfoil	20-50	pink	June to July
Myriophyllum verticillatum	whorled milfoil	20-50	pink	June to July
Potamogeton crispus	curled pondweed	50-100	-	-
Potamogeton lucens	shining pondweed	50-100	-	-
Ranunculus circinatus	spreading crowfoot	50-60	white	June to July
Utricularia vulgaris	greater bladderwort	10-80	yellow	June to August

When thinning the rampantly growing plant parts, you should not handle them too roughly, because even the smallest piece of shoot that breaks off will start to grow immediately and spread.

The greater bladderwort (*Utricularia vulgaris*) also makes do without roots. It is one of the carnivorous plants and uses the small bladders on the forked leaves to catch small animals living in the water, such as mosquito larvae, and transforms them into nutrients. The yellow flowers, which resemble those of the snapdragon, appear above the water from June to August and have a diameter of about two centimeters. Shallow riparian sites warmed by the sun offer the greater bladderwort **(illustration above right)** the best living conditions.

PLANTS FOR BOGS AND SHALLOW WATER

The plants that live in these zones, of which some parts are flooded by water, some are boggy, and others only moist, exhibit an amazing ability to adapt to the frequently changing conditions of their environment. Depending on the moisture supply, different kinds of leaves will develop. For example, thicker and smaller ones with few stomata will develop when the water supply is low. If such species reach deeper water, they develop submerged forms until they again extend large sections above the surface and take on their customary form.

The most familiar example of this adaptability is the creeping Jenny (*Lysimachia nummularia*). It grows in shallow water, in bogs, and in normal moist garden soil. The morningstar sedge (*Carex grayi*) is even less fussy

The greater bladderwort (*Utricularia vulgaris*).

Flat, low plants, like the creeping Jenny *(Lysimachia nummularia),* which serve to stabilize the bank, can overgrow the garden pond lining and thereby make it ineffective. This can be prevented through occasional trimming.

with respect to the moisture level. It feels equally at home in up to ten centimeters of standing water and in any other part of the garden away from the pond, even if the seeds have been carried away from it. Then the plant with the interesting, spiny seed heads accidentally becomes a "weed."

THE BOG GARDEN

Whether the bog garden adjoins the pond or a separate, somewhat more extensive zone of shallow water is selected, there is no lack of suitable plants that thrive in both places so that in this area the term water garden can be taken literally. It is not just narrow foliage plants like bulrushes *(Scirpus),* rushes

(Juncus), reeds, or sedges *(Carex)* which set the scene, but conspicuous flowering plants as well, which can make a sensation here.

In late March the yellow flowers of the marsh marigold *(Caltha palustris)* open, which herald the spring in small clumps beside or in the water. The pure-white flowers of the bog arum *(Calla palustris)* are displayed from June to August, and are followed later by the red, poisonous berries. Blooming at about the same time are the red trumpets of the marsh gladiolus *(Gladiolus palustris),* which does not, however,

like to stand directly in the water.

Japanese iris *(Iris kaempferi)*, bog iris *(Iris laevigata)*, and yellow flag *(Iris pseudacorus)*, **(illustrated on page 39)** brighten the scene starting in late May/early June with the drum roll of heavily veined pink, blue, violet, or yellow flowers. Depending on the species the flowering period lasts until August, so that with sufficient space it is possible to derive pleasure from these beautiful plants for most of the summer.

A mid-to-late-summer bloomer is the purple loosestrife (*Lythrum salicaria*, **illustration on page 39)** with 120-centimeter-high, red or violet flower stalks. These plants are found growing wild along the margins of natural bodies of water. Somewhat earlier, but also as late as September, the musks (*Mimulus* hybrids and *Mimulus ringens*) show the colorful spectrum of their often striped or spotted flowers, which

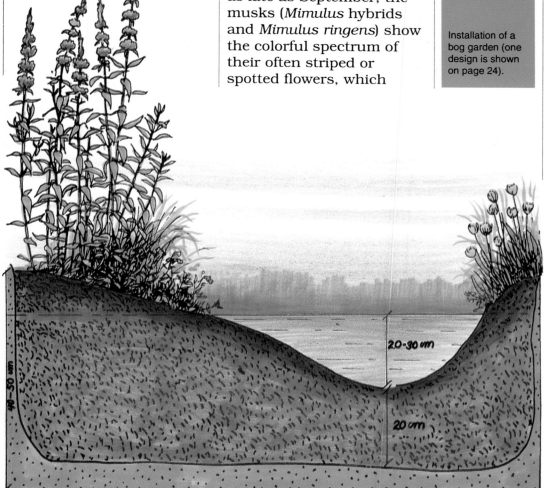

Installation of a bog garden (one design is shown on page 24).

20-30 cm

20 cm

resemble small orchids on closer inspection. They can turn over fairly large rocks on the water's edge as their shoots grow, and are often self-seeding.

The water forget-me-not *(Myosotis palustris)* has small, blue flowers with a yellow center, which brighten the water's edge from spring to late summer. When this species, which produces runners, likes its living conditions, it can form small, light-blue carpets.

How to create a bog garden is shown on page 20.

PLANTS FOR THE MARGINAL ZONE

With this group it is less a question of site than of design. With respect to the nature of the soil, the pond margin does not differ from the usual flower bed unless there is a natural body of water in the garden that supplies moisture to the soil in the bank region. On the other hand, artificial pools are supposed to retain their contents and at most act to raise the humidity slightly in their immediate vicinity, which is tolerated by most plants.

Because the pond represents a bit of living nature, this will usually be considered in the design of its immediate vicinity and the planting of cultivated perennials will as a rule be avoided. Naturally, the rule that "whatever you like is good" applies here too. The fact that unconventional solutions can also look good is shown by the example of the garden pond with summer flowers **(see page 13).**

The supply of wild perennials is varied enough to fulfill all wishes. Before you begin planting, however, you should think long and hard about what

A water lily situated in the marginal zone.

PLANTS FOR BOGS AND SHALLOW WATER

Botanical Name	Common Name	Water Depth in cm	Flower Color	Flowering Period
Acorus calamus	common sweet flag	5-20	green	June to July
Alisma plantago-aquatica	water plantain	10-30	white	June to September
Butomus umbellatus	flowering rush	5-20	pink	June to August
Calla palustris	bog arum	5-10	white	May to September
Caltha palustris	marsh marigold	bog	yellow	March to April
Carex grayi	morningstar sedge	0-10	green	June to July
Carex pseudocyperus	cyperus sedge	20-30	yellow	June to July
Cyperus longus	sweet galingale	bog	reddish brown	June to July
Eleocharis acicularis	hair grass	5-20	brown	June to July
Eriophorum species	cotton grass	bog	yellow/white/brown	April to August
Eupatorium purpureum	Joe-Pye weed	bog	red	July to September
Euphorbia palustris	water spurge	5-10	green	May to June
Filipendula ulmaria	meadow sweet	bog	white	June to August
Gentiana pneumonanthe	gentian	bog	blue	July to September
Gladiolus palustris	marsh gladiolus	bog	red	June to July
Hippuris vulgaris	common mare's tail	5-20	-	-
Iris kaempferi/ensata	Japanese iris	bog	blue/lilac/pink	June to July
Iris laevigata	bog iris	bog	blue	June to August
Iris pseudacorus	yellow flag	0-30	yellow	May to July
Iris versicolor	American yellow flag	bog	reddish violet	June to July
Juncus compressus	bulbous rush	bog	yellow-brown	June to August
Juncus effusus	soft rush	10-20	yellow-brown	June to August
Juncus ensifolius	dwarf rush	0-10	yellow-brown	June to August
Lysimachia nummularia	creeping Jenny	0-10	yellow	May to August
Lythrum salicaria	purple loosestrife	bog	red	July to September
Mentha aquatica	water mint	10-30	lilac	July to October
Menyanthes trifoliata	bog bean	5-30	white	April to May

goes where. Above all, the ultimate size of the plants must be considered, so that the view of the water will not be blocked. Tall perennial grasses, such as giant Chinese reed (*Miscanthus sinensis*), pipe grass (*Molinia caerulea*), or even bamboo species must be placed to the side or in the background, where their dominance is not disruptive. They should

PLANTS FOR BOGS AND SHALLOW WATER

Botanical Name	Common Name	Water Depth in cm	Flower Color	Flowering Period
Mimulus hybrids	musk	0-20	many colors	June to September
Mimulus lutens	yellow musk	0-5	yellow	June to August
Mimulus ringens	blue musk	0-20	blue	July to September
Myosotis palustris	water forget-me-not	5-10	blue	May to September
Myosotis rehsteineri	Lake Constanc forget-me-not	bog	blue	April to May
Onoclea sensibilis	sensitive fern	bog	-	-
Orontium aquaticum	golden club	5-40	yellow	April to May
Phragmites australis	spire reed	5-50	brown	July to September
Physostegia virginiana	false dragonhead	bog	white/pink	June to September
Pilularia globulifera	pill fern	bog	-	-
Pontederia cordata	pickerel weed	10-30	blue	July to August
Primula japonica	Japanese primula	bog	carmine	May to June
Primula rosea	rose primula	bog	pink	June to August
Ranunculus flammula	lesser spearwort	10-30	yellow	July to August
Ranunculus lingula	greater spearwort	10-30	yellow	July to August
Sagittaria latifolia	broad-leaved arrowhead	10-40	white	June to August
Sagittaria sagittifolia	arrowhead	10-40	white	June to August
Scirpus lacustris	bulrush	20-100	brown	June to July
Scirpus taberaemontani "Zebrinus"	zebra rush	20-100	brown	June to July
Solanum dulcamara	bittersweet	bog	violet	June to August
Sparganium erectum	branched bur reed	20-40	green	June to August
Sparganium minimum	lesser bur reed	10-30	white	June to August
Thelypteris palustris	bog kidney fern	bog	-	-
Typha angustifolia	narrow-leaved cattail	30-50	brown	June to July
Typha latifolia	broad-leaved cattail	20-50	brown	June to July
Typha minima	dwarf cattail	10-20	brown	May to September
Veronica beccabunga	brooklime	0-5	blue	May to August

rather represent an additional focal point. The same is true of large flowering perennials, such as goat's beard (Aruncus dioicus), snakeroot (Cimicifuga racemosa), coneflower (Echinacea purpurea), perennial sunflower (Helianthus salicifolius), or ligularia (Ligularia przewalskii).

As with other perennial plantings, the flowering period and color finally also play an important, creative role. Naturally, the border should bloom as long and continuously as possible, and the colors must not clash too harshly or similarly colored flowers be placed so close together that the individual blossoms can barely be distinguished. On the other hand, in nature there are comparatively few incompatible gradations of color, and sensible gardening in the traditional English style is in any case out of place in the pond area.

Bamboo and other invasive grasses can penetrate the liner with their very hard, very sharp subterranean shoots (rhizomes).

A SMALL SELECTION OF PLANTS FOR THE MARGINAL ZONE

Botanical Name	Common Name	Water Depth in cm	Flower Color	Flowering Period
Athyrium filix-femina	lady fern	60-70	-	-
Adiantum pedatum	maidenhair fern	20-40	-	-
Ajuga reptans	bugle	20-30	blue	April to June
Alchemilla vulgaris	lady's mantle	30-40	green-yellow	June to August
Anemone X Japonica hybrids	Japanese windflower	60-80	white/pink	July to September
Arabis caucasica	rock cress	10-20	white	April to May
Aruncus dioicus	goat's beard	80-120	white	June to July
Astilbe species and varieties	garden spirea	50-80	white/pink/red	July to August
Bergenia cordifolia	bergenia	20-30	pink	April to May
Blechnum spicant	ribbed fern	20-30	-	-
Brunnera macrophylla	alkanet	40-60	blue	April to June
Cardamine pratensis	cuckoo flower	10-30	pale lilac	April to June
Cimicifuga racemosa	snakeroot	120-200	white	August to September
Doronicum caucasicum	leopardbane	50-60	yellow	April to May
Dryas octopetala	dryas	2-10	white	June to August
Echinacea purpurea	purple loosestrife	60-100	red	July to September
Festuca glauca	festuca	10-20	blue-green	May to June
Fritillaria meleagris	checkerboard fritillaria	20-30	purple/white	from April
Gentiana septemfida	gentian	10-15	dark-blue	July to September
Geranium pratense	crane's bill	50-60	light-blue	June to July
Helianthus salicifolius	perennial sunflower	180-250	yellow	September to October
Hemerocallis varieties	daylily	70-80	yellow/brown/rusty red	June to August
Hosta species	plaintain lily	30-60	light-blue	July to August
Inula magnifica	inula	150-250	yellow	July to September
Iris chrysographes	iris chrysographes	40-60	violet/blackish red	June
Iris forrestii	iris forrestii	50	yellow/brown	June to July
Iris sibirica	Siberian iris	60-80	blue	May to June
Iris wilsonii	iris wilsonii	60-70	yellow	May to June
Kniphofia uvaria	red hot poker	60-80	red-yellow	July to August
Liatris spicata	gayfeather	60-80	lilac-pink	July to August
Ligularia przewalskii	ligularia	100-140	yellow	July to August
Lychnis viscaria	campion	50	red/pink	June to July
Lysimachia punctata	loosestrife	60-100	yellow	July to August
Miscanthus sinensis	giant Chinese reed	180-300	-	-
Molinia caerulea	pipe grass	100-120	brownish red	September to October
Osmunda regalis	royal fern	80-120	-	-
Pennisetum alopecuroides	lamp cleaner grass	50-80	reddish green	August to October
Phyllitis scolopendrium	stag's tongue fern	30-40	-	-
Phyllostachys aurea	bamboo	300-400	-	-
Polemonium caeruleum	Jacob's ladder	50-70	blue/white	June to August
Primula denticulata	drumstick primula	10-20	pink	February to April
Primula florindae	Himalayan cowslip	40-50	yellow	June to August
Primula veris	key primula	15-25	yellow	April to May
Pulmonaria angustifolia	lung weed	10-20	blue	March to April
Rudbeckia fulgida	coneflower	40-70	yellow	August to October
Stipa barbata	feather grass	60-80	reddish white	June to August
Tradescantia X Andersoniana hybrids	spiderwort	40-60	blue/white	June to July
Trollius europaeus	globe flower	30-50	yellow	May to June